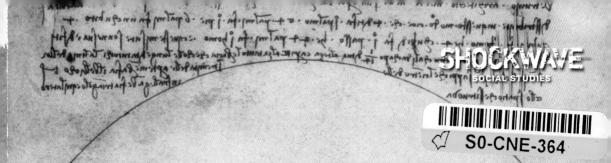

S0-CNE-364

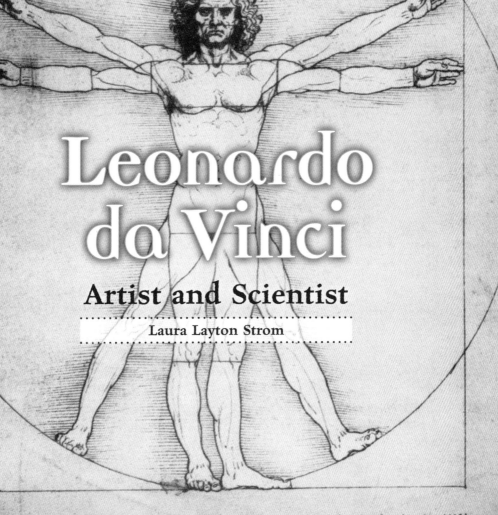

Leonardo da Vinci

Artist and Scientist

Laura Layton Strom

children's press®

An imprint of Scholastic Inc.
NEW YORK • TORONTO • LONDON • AUCKLAND • SYDNEY
MEXICO CITY • NEW DELHI • HONG KONG
DANBURY, CONNECTICUT

Library of Congress Cataloging-in-Publication Data
Strom, Laura Layton, 1962-
   Leonardo da Vinci : artist and scientist / by Laura Layton Strom.
       p. cm. -- (Shockwave)
   Includes index.
   ISBN 10: 0-531-17771-8 (lib. bdg.)
   ISBN 13: 978-0-531-17771-6 (lib. bdg.)
   ISBN 10: 0-531-18798-5 (lib. pbk.)
   ISBN 13: 978-0-531-18798-2 (lib. pbk.)
1. Leonardo, da Vinci, 1452-1519--Juvenile literature. 2.
Artists--Italy--Biography--Juvenile literature. 3.
Scientists--Italy--Biography--Juvenile literature. I. Leonardo, da
Vinci, 1452-1519. II. Title. III. Series.

   N6923.L33.S77 2007
   709.2--dc22
   [B]
2007008936

Published in 2008 by Children's Press, an imprint of Scholastic Inc.,
557 Broadway, New York, New York 10012
www.scholastic.com

08 09 10 11 12 13 14 15 16 17
10 9 8 7 6 5 4 3 2 1

Printed in China through Colorcraft Ltd., Hong Kong

Author: Laura Layton Strom
Editor: Mary Atkinson
Designer: Matthew Alexander
Photo Researcher: Jamshed Mistry

Photographs by: Getty Images (ad for *The Da Vinci Code* movie);
Jennifer and Brian Lupton (children, pp. 30–31); **Photolibrary** (cover; crowds
at the Louvre, p. 17; p. 20; skeleton studies, p. 21; p. 24; anatomical study,
pp. 30–31); **Topfoto: www.stockcentral.co.nz** (p. 25); **Tranz/Corbis** (p. 1;
p. 5; pp. 6–16; the *Mona Lisa*, p. 17; pp. 18–19; anatomical study of an arm,
p. 21; pp. 22–23; heart diagram, p. 25; pp. 26–28; fantasy drawing, p. 29)

All illustrations and other photographs © Weldon Owen Education Inc.

CONTENTS

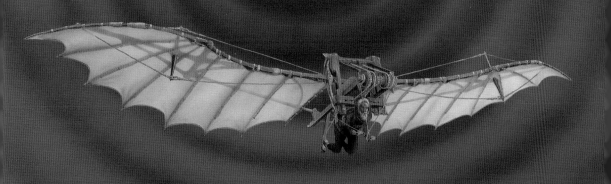

masterpiece an outstanding work of art or craft

medieval (*med ee EE vuhl*) to do with the Middle Ages

Middle Ages the period in European history from about 500 A.D. to about 1500 A.D.

perspective the art of drawing or painting a scene so that forms and objects appear to have the same shapes and relative sizes as they do in real life. For example, distant objects are smaller than nearer ones.

Renaissance (*REN uh sahnts*) the period in European history that began in Italy in about 1300 and lasted until about 1600. The Renaissance (meaning "rebirth") was marked by advances in art, literature, and science.

. . . .

For easy reference, see Wordmark on back flap.
For additional vocabulary, see Glossary on page 32.

Medieval — many words have a root word or cluster of root letters that give a clue to their meaning. The root letters *ev* relate to age or time. Words with this cluster include *medieval*, *ever*, and *evolution*. You may be able to think of some others.

A **perspective** study for
Adoration of the Magi,
an unfinished work
by Leonardo da Vinci

Leonardo da Vinci was one of the greatest artists of all time. He was also an early scientist. However, his scientific work was not understood until long after he died.

Leonardo was born in Italy. He lived at the end of the **Middle Ages**. This was a time when most learning had to do with religion. Leonardo also lived at the beginning of the **Renaissance**. This was when Europeans began to study the world around them. They began to advance ideas in science, art, and literature. Leonardo was more of a "Renaissance man" than someone living in the Middle Ages. He passionately questioned why and how things happened.

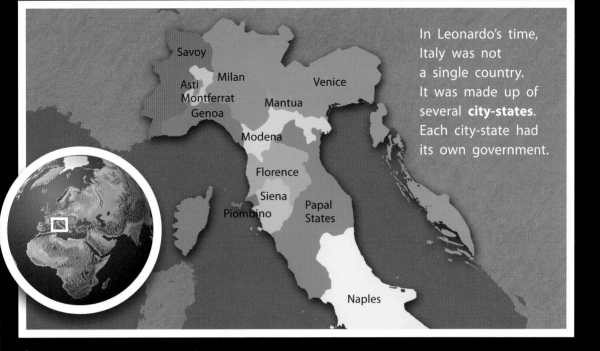

Savoy

Asti
Montferrat
Genoa

Milan

Mantua

Venice

Modena

Florence

Siena

Piombino

Papal
States

Naples

In Leonardo's time,
Italy was not
a single country.
It was made up of
several **city-states**.
Each city-state had
its own government.

As an artist, Leonardo produced two of the world's best-known
paintings: *Mona Lisa* and *The Last Supper*. As a scientist,
he made many discoveries and thought up many inventions
long before other scientists did. However, he didn't publish his
ideas. Perhaps this was because people were not yet ready
to accept them.

Detail from *The Last Supper*,
by Leonardo da Vinci

Black Death

The Middle Ages were violent and primitive by our standards. People who questioned laws were beaten or killed. Few people owned books or could read. Most people didn't wash often. They didn't understand the need for **hygiene**. City streets were piled with stinking waste. Rats lived in many homes. **Plagues** killed thousands of people. During the black-death **epidemic** of 1348, one in every three people died! Even at other times, most people lived short lives. If diseases didn't kill them, medical treatments did. Patients were sliced open to release "bad blood." Surgery was done by barbers. It often led to death from bleeding, shock, or infection.

In the Middle Ages, some people thought that dancing would make God spare them from the plague.

and Bad Blood

SHOCKER

In the Middle Ages, people stuffed pig manure up their noses to stop nose bleeds.

This medieval drawing shows the inside of the body. People's knowledge of the body was based on very little actual examination.

In **medieval** Europe, people did not look for scientific reasons for the things that happened. Bad blood, **supernatural** powers, and the stars were said to cause society's ills. Most people accepted these explanations. However, by the 1400s in Italy, things were beginning to change. The Renaissance had begun. Leonardo da Vinci was part of the changes. Leonardo questioned everything!

A Hard Start

The house near Vinci
where Leonardo grew up

The heading "A Hard Start" suggests that these pages will probably be about Leonardo's early life. Knowing what to expect makes the text easier to read.

Leonardo was born near Vinci, a town in Florence. In fact, the name *da Vinci* means "from Vinci." Leonardo's parents were not married. Leonardo lived with his father's family. He later had several stepmothers and many half brothers and sisters. As he grew up, he spent a lot of time alone. Leonardo always carried a notebook. He enjoyed drawing things he saw in nature.

Leonardo was not allowed to attend university or to work in a top profession. This was because his parents hadn't married. Leonardo didn't let this hold him back. He decided to make up for these unfair rules by reading everything he could. Leonardo's father noticed his son's artistic talent. He helped Leonardo get a lucky break – a job with Andrea del Verrocchio, a master artist.

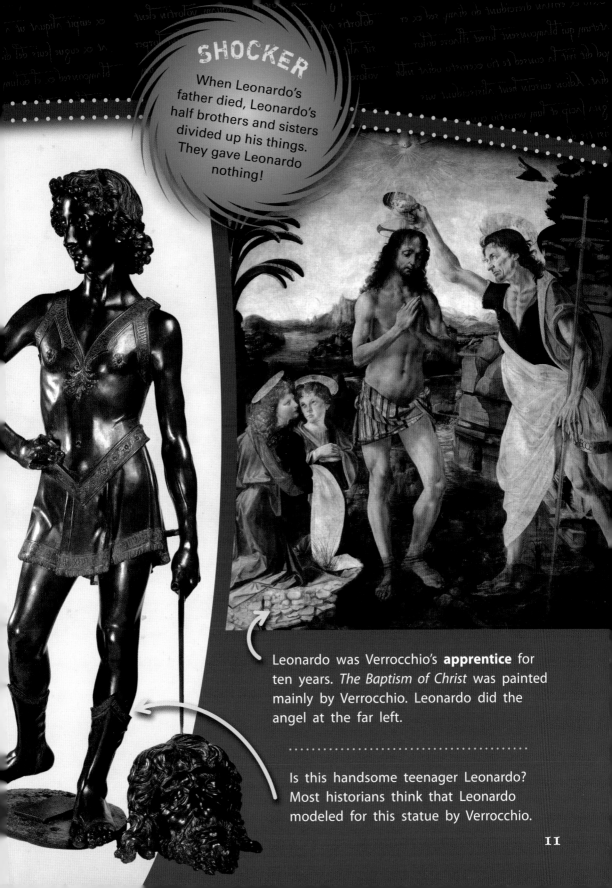

Leonardo was Verrocchio's **apprentice** for ten years. *The Baptism of Christ* was painted mainly by Verrocchio. Leonardo did the angel at the far left.

Is this handsome teenager Leonardo? Most historians think that Leonardo modeled for this statue by Verrocchio.

Early Work

Leonardo studied math as a young artist. This helped him use **perspective** to make his paintings look realistic. Leonardo also **dissected** animals to learn more about their structures. For fun, he sometimes joined body parts from different animals into creepy combinations, such as lizard-bats. Verrocchio encouraged dissection among his apprentices. He wanted complete accuracy in their work. He also encouraged them to make plaster casts of their own body parts and of corpse body parts. The apprentices used them to help make realistic sculptures.

Leonardo always preferred sketching ideas to finishing his artworks.

Louis I, Duke of Anjou, by Johansen Krause, 1300s

Leonardo's *Lady With an Ermine*, 1480s

SHOCKER

Leonardo liked to put bits of dead animals in other artists' equipment to shock them.

The portrait on the left is from the Middle Ages. The one on the right is an example of Renaissance art. Which one seems more realistic? Why do you think this is?

Leonardo worked hard, but rarely finished his work. He toyed with designs for new machines. Leonardo was easily distracted. He jumped from project to project. Historians say Leonardo left behind more undone work than any other artist.

Leonardo was disorganized and messy. He had trouble concentrating on one thing for long. However, he was quick-minded and had a wonderful imagination. He was also curious, sensitive, and polite.

When Leonardo finished his training, he needed to find work. Since the Italian city-states were at war, he decided that designing war machines might be a good bet. He later came to despise war. However at this stage, the challenge of designing war machines excited him. He designed guns, submarines, and many other things. They were far ahead of their time, but most were never built.

In 1481, Leonardo was passed over as an artist for the Sistine Chapel in Rome. Angry that the **Pope** had not chosen him for this **prestigious** job, he decided it was time for a change. In 1482, he moved to Milan. There he got a job as a military engineer and architect.

The black death led Leonardo to study hygiene and **sanitation**. Italy's city streets were filled with human waste. Leonardo concluded that waste carries diseases into drinking water. He made a plan for a healthy city. It had plumbing, street cleaning, and public toilets.

> I wasn't sure what *passed over* meant, so I just kept reading. The next sentence made the meaning clearer. I read the first again and it made sense.

Leonardo had a sense of humor. He was fascinated by unusual features as well as beautiful ones.

Sickness

Some of Leonardo's designs for war machines, including a "tank"

The plague struck Italy many times during the Middle Ages and Renaissance. Leonardo, however, escaped the disease.

15

Masterpieces

In 1495, Leonardo began a project now considered a **masterpiece**. It was *The Last Supper*. He painted this giant mural on the walls of a **monastery** dining hall. He painted for days at a time. Sometimes he forgot to eat. Leonardo used a new method of painting that he had invented himself. Unfortunately, the paint soon began to flake off. Experts have worked to keep the painting visible. But, sadly, not much of the original paint remains.

I now know that
The Last Supper:
- is a masterpiece
- is a giant mural
- used a new painting method
- is in poor condition

The Last Supper

In 1503, Leonardo created another masterpiece – *Mona Lisa*. The woman in the painting has an unusual, irregular smile. The smile has intrigued people ever since it was first painted. The painting must have been very special to Leonardo. He kept it near him for the rest of his life.

Mona Lisa

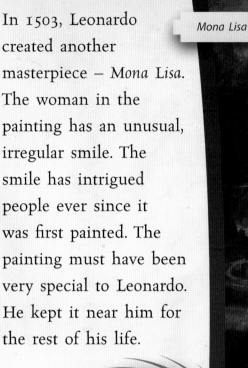

SHOCKER

No one knows for sure who posed for *Mona Lisa*. Some people have suggested that it was Leonardo himself!

When Leonardo died, his apprentice, Salai, inherited *Mona Lisa*. When Salai died in 1523, *Mona Lisa* was bought by the French king. It is now in the Louvre (*LOO vruh*), a museum in Paris. There it attracts large crowds every day.

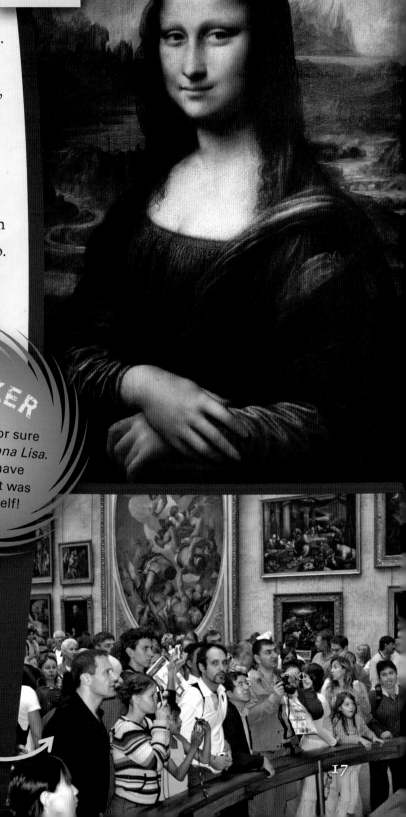

The Secret Notebooks

Leonardo often wondered about things that others took for granted. Why is the sky blue? What causes vomiting? How do birds fly? Sometimes he tested his ideas. He wrote down his predictions, did experiments, and then wrote conclusions. This was an early use of what later developed into the **scientific method**.

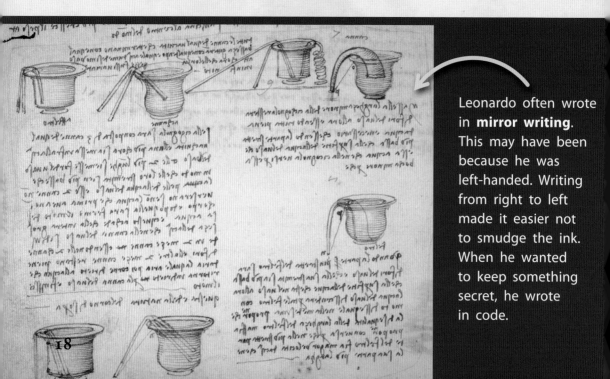

Leonardo often wrote in **mirror writing**. This may have been because he was left-handed. Writing from right to left made it easier not to smudge the ink. When he wanted to keep something secret, he wrote in code.

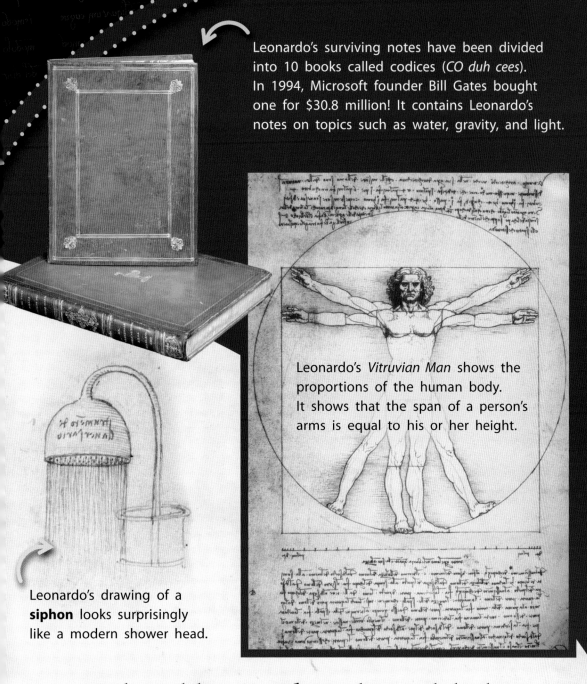

Leonardo's surviving notes have been divided into 10 books called codices (*CO duh cees*). In 1994, Microsoft founder Bill Gates bought one for $30.8 million! It contains Leonardo's notes on topics such as water, gravity, and light.

Leonardo's *Vitruvian Man* shows the proportions of the human body. It shows that the span of a person's arms is equal to his or her height.

Leonardo's drawing of a **siphon** looks surprisingly like a modern shower head.

Leonardo jotted down every **theory**, design, and idea that came into his head. Often he wrote through the night. His notebooks became his reason for living. Sadly, the people who later inherited the notebooks didn't realize what they had. They lost about three-quarters of them! Most of the 13,000 surviving pages went unread for years.

The Bodies of the Dead

Leonardo kept much of his scientific work private. He may have worried about being laughed at, or worse, being thrown into prison. The dissection work he did was illegal. Because of this, Leonardo worked at night. Historians think that he dissected more than 30 bodies, mostly of criminals. Leonardo believed that the human body was the ultimate machine. He wanted to know how the skeleton linked up. He wanted to know how blood flowed, and how muscles worked. He was the first person to:

- explain the skeletal system correctly
- discover hardened **arteries** as a cause of death
- report that the heart is a muscle that pumps blood
- draw a human baby inside its mother's body

SHOCKER

In the 15th century, neither refrigeration nor chemical preservatives existed. Bodies decayed quickly. Leonardo had to work fast or risk throwing up from the stink.

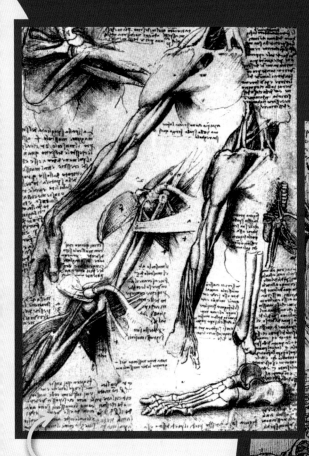

Leonardo sketched the body parts he studied, including muscles (above) and bones (right). His drawings look more like modern medical drawings than medieval ones (see page 9).

The *il-* prefix is used to form opposites: legal/ illegal, logical/illogical.

21

Slimy Eyeballs

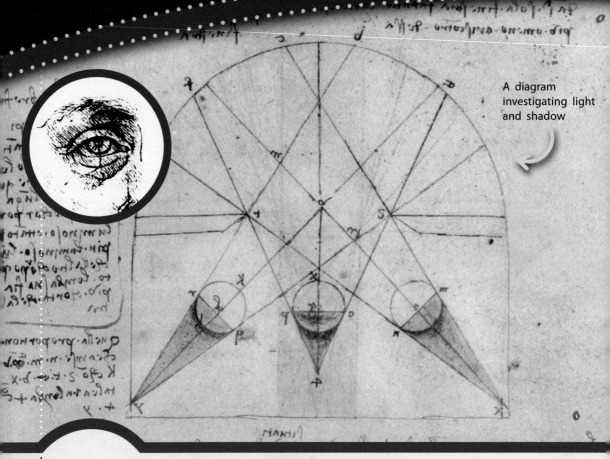

A diagram investigating light and shadow

Most people in Leonardo's time accepted the theories of the ancient Greeks. Some of the ancient Greeks had written that the eye sends light rays to the objects it sees. Leonardo, however, questioned these theories. He was fascinated with eyes and vision. He made models with mirrors, glass balls, and lenses to figure out how the eye works. He even discussed the idea of contact lenses.

To study eyeballs more easily, Leonardo needed to make them easier to cut. He hard-boiled them like eggs. This made them less slimy and mushy.

Leonardo studied light, reflection, and shadows in great detail. He designed a device for viewing a solar eclipse safely. He also wrote about the idea of using mirrors and lenses to magnify the moon and planets. Yet the first telescope was not invented until a century later.

Leonardo also studied animals' eyes. He realized that animals that feed at night have larger eyes than brains. Other land animals usually have smaller eyes than brains.

Water and Wings

Water fascinated Leonardo. He made notes about it and about how to control it. He made drawings of watercraft and diving suits. He even made plans for very wide, flat shoes that could be used to walk on water.

Leonardo yearned to fly. He had learned to swim by copying frogs. So he tried to fly by studying birds, bats, and flying insects. He designed many different flying machines. Historians disagree as to whether he actually made any of them. Although some were well designed, they were too heavy to actually fly. However, Leonardo is credited with designing the first parachute.

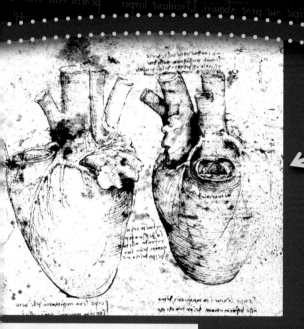

Not all of Leonardo's theories were completely correct. For example, he rightly said that the heart pumps blood through the body. However, he wrongly concluded that rivers contain a heart that pumps water!

Leonardo drew this sketch of his idea for a life preserver.

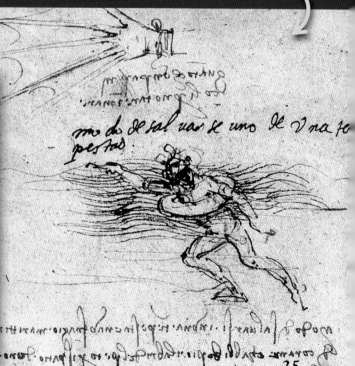

Some of these innovations were first dreamed up by Leonardo but never published by him.

- Steam power, 1698

- Parachute, 1783

- Bicycle, 1790

- Helicopter, 1907

- Robot, 1921

- Solar panels, 1954

By 1500, Leonardo had spent so much time on his notebooks that he had little money. He began moving from town to town, taking on paying jobs. He mostly designed machines, gardens, home improvements, and toys. Sometimes he was hired to draw maps.

In his later years, Leonardo moved to Rome to work for the Pope. When he wasn't working, he studied plants in the beautiful Vatican gardens. He was also allowed to do **autopsies** on those who died at the local hospital. However, this work made him unpopular. Some people thought it meant he was involved in witchcraft.

I remember reading that people in the Middle Ages were very **superstitious**. Maybe that's why people thought autopsies were related to witchcraft.

The building in France where Leonardo last lived is now a museum honoring him.

Leonardo's last job took him to France. He became Premier Painter, Engineer, and Architect for King Francis I. He worked until his eyesight failed, his teeth fell out, and he became paralyzed by a stroke. In 1519, he died. He was 67 years old.

Some of Leonardo's last drawings were nightmarish pictures of the end of the world. Psychiatrists think he knew that he was close to death and was fearful of it.

Leonardo left behind astonishing drawings and paintings. He also described scientific ideas and inventions far beyond anything others were producing at that time. Here are a few of his many ideas that others later improved or invented themselves.

- The first accurate drawings of anatomy.
  These are credited to Dr. Andreas Vesalius (1543).

- The theory that Earth revolves around the sun.
  This is credited to astronomer Nicolaus Copernicus (1543).

- The law that states that objects at rest tend to remain at rest, originally called Leonardo's Law. Today, we call this Newton's first law of motion. Scientist Isaac Newton published the law nearly 200 years later, in 1687.

- Flying machines.
  These are credited to the Wright Brothers (1903).

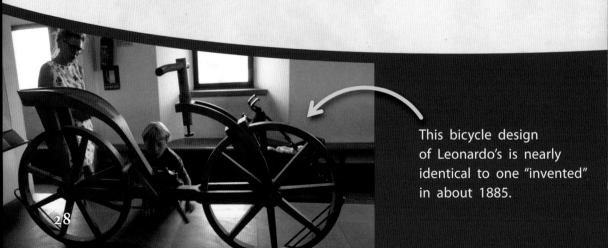

This bicycle design of Leonardo's is nearly identical to one "invented" in about 1885.

Ahead of the Pack

Some of Leonardo's drawings came mainly from his imagination.

Today, many people assume that science and art cannot mix. They think that a person is either good at science and math or good at creative subjects. Leonardo is proof that works of great genius can emerge from the combination of art and science.

Many people have been inspired by Leonardo. *The Da Vinci Code* is a best-selling novel by Dan Brown. It has also been made into a movie. In the story, someone is murdered. The body is posed like Leonardo's *Vitruvian Man*. The paintings *Mona Lisa* and *The Last Supper* supposedly contain clues to solving the crime.

Leonardo loved nature. He studied it with awe and with a scientific mind. He was a vegetarian in a time when almost everyone ate meat. He believed that all creatures that moved felt pain. He even despised hunting. However, Leonardo also cut up dead bodies to study them, which was against the law.

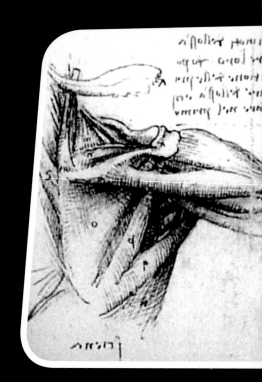

WHAT DO YOU THINK?

Do you think Leonardo was right to cut up bodies illegally?

PRO

Leonardo had to break the law. There was no other way he could learn about the body. The people were dead, so they felt no pain. He was doing important work that improved his art. It also could have improved medicine if he had published his work.

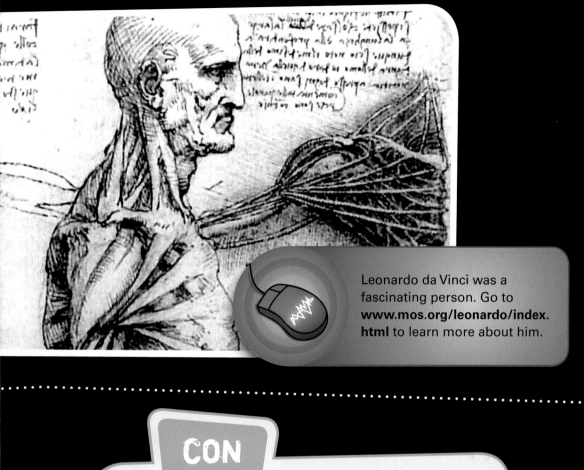

Leonardo da Vinci was a fascinating person. Go to **www.mos.org/leonardo/index. html** to learn more about him.

CON

I think it was disrespectful and disgusting. The people had not given permission for him to do that work. It was illegal, and laws are made for a reason. If people could take dead bodies anytime, there would be less respect for the dead.

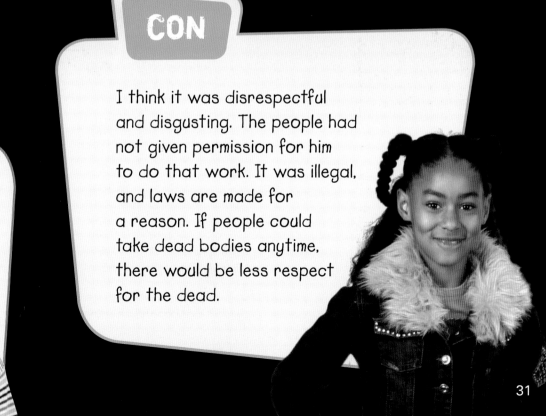

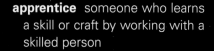

apprentice someone who learns a skill or craft by working with a skilled person

artery a blood vessel that carries blood away from the heart

autopsy (*AW top see*) the study of a body to figure out the cause of death

city-state a city and its surrounding area that functions like a nation with its own government

dissect to cut the tissue of an organism in order to study its structure

epidemic a disease that spreads quickly

hygiene (*HI jeen*) conditions and practices that improve health and cleanliness

mirror writing writing that reads from right to left and has letters that face the wrong way. Mirror writing looks like ordinary writing in a mirror.

monastery a place where monks live and work

plague (*PLAYG*) a disease, especially the black death, or bubonic plague, that spreads quickly and kills many people

Pope the leader of the Roman Catholic Church

prestigious something that brings respect and high status

sanitation systems for keeping water clean and getting rid of sewage

scientific method a way of gaining scientific knowledge by observing, experimenting, and analyzing results

siphon (*SYE fuhn*) a bent tube through which water can be made to flow

supernatural to do with things that cannot be described with natural laws or normal understanding

superstitious a belief in supernatural things, such as witchcraft

theory an idea about why something happens

· ·